MetLife Foundation PRESENTS

MOORE
IN AMERICA

Monumental Sculpture at The New York Botanical Garden

Moore at the Hermann Noack bronze foundry in Berlin with a cast in
progress of *Large Two Forms* 1966
photo: The Henry Moore Foundation archive

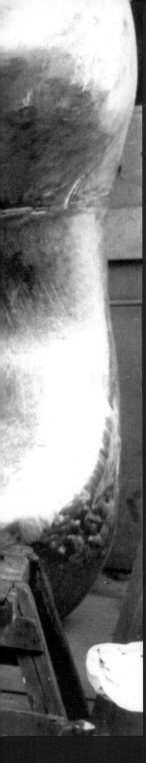

Contributors
Gregory Long
Richard Calvocoressi
Todd Forrest
David Finn
Anita Feldman

Principal Photography
David Finn

Editorial Direction
Sally Armstrong Leone
Carol Capobianco

Creative Direction
Terry Skoda

Graphic Design
Susan Siegrist

CO-CURATED WITH
The Henry Moore
Foundation

MetLife Foundation

MetLife Foundation is proud to present a landmark exhibition by the internationally acclaimed sculptor Henry Moore. *Moore in America: Monumental Sculpture at The New York Botanical Garden*, on display from May 24 to November 2, 2008, is the largest outdoor exhibition of Moore's work ever presented in the United States.

This unique show, installed across 250 acres, combines large-scale sculpture with the captivating landscape of the Botanical Garden. It provides visitors with an opportunity to witness and be inspired by Moore's iconic pieces in changing seasons and natural settings.

Underlying the work of MetLife Foundation is a long-standing commitment to access and opportunity. *Moore in America* exemplifies MetLife Foundation's mission of making the arts accessible. In addition, the many programs the Foundation supports help provide young people with the skills they need to succeed, create opportunities for people of all ages, strengthen communities, and address the issues of aging.

Sibyl Jacobson
President and
Chief Executive Officer
MetLife Foundation

MetLife Foundation PRESENTS
*Moore in America: Monumental Sculpture at
The New York Botanical Garden*

Exhibitions in the Enid A. Haupt Conservatory are made possible by the Estate of Enid A. Haupt.

Exhibitions in the Mertz Library are made possible by the LuEsther T. Mertz Charitable Trust, William D. Rondina and The Carlisle Collection, and The Kurt Berliner Foundation.

The New York Botanical Garden
Bronx, New York 10458–5126
www.nybg.org

The Henry Moore Foundation
Perry Green, Hertfordshire, UK
www.henry-moore-fdn.co.uk

ISBN 10: 0-89327-971-4
ISBN 13: 978-0-89327-971-4
©2008

Table of Contents

Sculpture Exhibited

Moore in 1979 with plaster *Working Model for Reclining Figure:
Angles* 1975–77 and its full-size enlargement
photo: The Henry Moore Foundation archive

Locking Piece (detail) 1963–64
photo: The Henry Moore Foundation archive

I am very pleased to welcome you to *Moore in America: Monumental Sculpture at The New York Botanical Garden*, the largest outdoor exhibition of Henry Moore's sculpture ever presented in a single venue in the United States. We extend our appreciation to the Henry Moore Foundation for its co-curation of the exhibition, which is underwritten by MetLife Foundation and travels to the Atlanta Botanical Garden in spring 2009.

The 20 colossal works displayed throughout The New York Botanical Garden provide for an impressive interaction of nature and art such as Moore envisioned. The beginnings of the Botanical Garden's enchanting landscape along the Bronx River, framed in forest and rock outcrops of varied topography, have a geological history shaped by natural forces. With a foundation of gneiss and schist, the river and marshland margins were a route and area of seasonal habitation for native peoples and European settlement. This ongoing relationship between nature and culture yielded the Garden landscape that became the palette for the form and complexity that exists today.

Henry Moore was raised in Yorkshire in the north of England, a pastiche of pasture and forest, of rolling hills and deep valleys. The interplay between the solid land forms and the void of sky must have made an indelible impression on him. Many of his larger works feel like landscapes themselves. Moore intended that his monumental works be presented in expansive settings so that their mass and size could be seen from many angles, in great variety of light, and in differing seasons. The New York Botanical Garden fits his intent perfectly, offering sweeping, undulating terrain, diverse plant collections, and magnificent gardens with the appropriate scale and beauty to complement his sculpture, as captured through the lens of David Finn in this catalog.

The Botanical Garden has been a premier cultural, research, and education institution since its founding in the early 1890s. In those formative years, this particular site was chosen because of the natural features, beauty, and diversity of its landscape. Today, the sculpture across the Garden once again focuses attention on the dramatic landscape and provides a perfect seasonal complement to the unparalleled year-round flower shows in the Enid A. Haupt Conservatory, America's preeminent Victorian-style glasshouse.

I hope that visitors will experience a newly found appreciation for Henry Moore's sculpture and The New York Botanical Garden. When viewed together, both are transformed.

The New York Botanical Garden is the ideal natural setting for Henry Moore's sculpture—romantic yet accessible to the public. All the works in this exhibition come from the last three decades of Moore's life, when he developed and refined his language of monumental forms suitable for siting in open landscape. Several originated in ideas worked out years earlier, such as *Large Reclining Figure* 1984, which was enlarged from a tiny lead sculpture of 1938 in the collection of the Museum of Modern Art in New York.

Moore first experimented with placing his sculpture outdoors in Scotland in the 1950s. This was not the Highlands but a landscape of gentle moorland, trees, rocks, and water, similar to the mixture of low hills, rock outcrops, and woodland that characterizes The New York Botanical Garden.

Cleverly sited, his works maintain a dialogue with the rock, tree, and plant forms found here. With the changes in light, level, and vegetation and the sense of discovery that the Garden encourages, visitors experience something almost magical as they move around.

It is a happy coincidence that the Botanical Garden has just celebrated Charles Darwin's contribution to botany prior to *Moore in America*. Darwin and Moore: two great Englishmen, one a natural scientist, the other an artist inspired by nature. The Henry Moore Foundation is proud to be associated with the Garden's efforts to bridge the gap between art and science.

Introduction
Richard Calvocoressi
Director
The Henry Moore Foundation

Moore inspecting a cast of *Oval with Points* 1968–70
photo: The Henry Moore Foundation archive

Foreword

Todd Forrest
Vice President for Horticulture
and Living Collections
The New York Botanical Garden

Henry Moore at Perry Green with
Mother and Child 1949
photo: The Henry Moore Foundation archive

Moore in America: Monumental Sculpture at The New York Botanical Garden is the perfect union of fine art and powerful landscape. Where better to see 20 pieces of Moore's sculpture than in a landscape that itself has been sculpted by glaciers and generations of gardeners? What better complement to a 250-acre National Historic Landmark than monumental sculpture inspired by natural forms? To see Moore's work at the Botanical Garden is to gain insight into both the artist's creations and his inspiration.

How does an exhibition of this magnitude evolve? In 2007 I had the great pleasure of walking through the Garden with curators Anita Feldman and David Mitchinson of the Henry Moore Foundation to finalize site selection for the sculpture. Anita and David had scouted the Garden the previous day and were eager to share their enthusiasm with me. Their delight in the Garden's dramatic hills and valleys punctuated by bold rock outcrops and shaded by towering trees was palpable and inspired me to see the Garden as Henry Moore might have. Around every curve was another potential location for one of Moore's great works.

With so many options, how does one choose where to place 20 sculptures that each weigh up to five tons? As we traveled through the Garden, Anita and David rotated each piece in their minds, careful to put both the sculpture and the landscape in the best light. They considered how the public would approach each sculpture and how the surrounding rocks, turf, and trees would emphasize certain qualities of the work. Together we considered how we could place the sculpture in a way that would introduce our visitors to the many wonders of the Garden, from the Arthur and Janet Ross Conifer Arboretum and the Benenson Ornamental Conifers to the Peggy Rockefeller Rose Garden and the Enid A. Haupt Conservatory.

There were also practical considerations: Henry Moore's works are large, and many needed to be lifted in place with cranes or maneuvered with large machines. We were careful to make sure that the sculpture could be placed without damaging sensitive areas of the Garden. We worked with art handler Frank Mariano, an expert in moving priceless (and heavy) works of art, to create an installation plan that would not impact our stewardship of the Garden or its living collections.

The careful planning paid off. Moore's sculpture feels at home in the Garden, perhaps because of the essential role that landscape played in their creation.

Henry Moore said, "The thing is that sculpture gains by finding a setting that suits its mood, and when that happens, there is gain for both sculpture and setting." *Moore in America: Monumental Sculpture at The New York Botanical Garden* truly proves this point.

In 1958 my wife, Laura, and I bought a small Henry Moore maquette from the Hanover Gallery in London. We also had an opportunity to visit Henry Moore and his wife, Irina, and their young daughter, Mary, at their home in Much Hadham. In the following years, we visited the Moores every time we went to London, and we became close friends.

When we bought a large sculpture called *Bridge Prop* (which we later donated to Brown University), I took more than 100 photographs of the sculpture to show Henry how much we appreciated its wonderful forms. So pleased, he urged me to publish a book with those photographs to show people how to look at sculpture. I did with *As the Eye Moves*.

Moore once said that a person can have a very different experience seeing the same sculpture in different locations. He especially loved seeing his works in natural environments where they could be related to rocks and trees and the sky above.

That inspired me to think of photographing Henry Moore's sculpture in public places around the world. Henry was delighted with the idea, and I photographed his sculpture in Japan, Australia, Israel, France, Italy, Switzerland, Germany, the Netherlands, Belgium, Denmark, Sweden, England, Scotland, Ireland, Canada, and the United States. The photographs were published by Harry Abrams in a book called *Henry Moore, Sculpture and Environment*.

In 1993 an exhibition at the Yale Center for British Art of my photographs of Henry Moore sculpture had the unusual title, *One Man's Henry Moore*. The director, Duncan Robinson, thought that the title would express the close relationship as a photographer and a friend that I had with Henry Moore for so many years.

Moore's reputation rose to great heights during his lifetime. Art historian Kenneth Clark once told me that Moore was the greatest sculptor of the 20th century. And I heard art critic Herbert Read give a speech at the New School in New York in which he said that the four greatest sculptors in history were Phidias, Michelangelo, Rodin, and Moore. I later told that to Henry and he laughed embarrassedly, but since I had photographed most of the works of all four artists for books on their sculpture, I didn't disagree.

Over the past 40 years I have published books on Egyptian, Greek, Roman, Medieval, Renaissance, Baroque, 20th century, Asian, and pre-Columbian works, and I have no doubt that Moore deserves to be included in the top of any list of the greatest sculptors in all periods. It was a privilege, therefore, for me to photograph his work once again, in the ideal setting of The New York Botanical Garden.

Original bone and plasticine maquette for *Working Model for Standing Figure: Knife Edge* 1961
photo: John Hedgecoe

"Sculpture is an art of the open

to it, and for me its best settin

I would rather have a piece of r

almost any landscape, than in, o

I know." —Moore, 1951

. Daylight, sunlight, is necessary

nd complement is nature.

sculpture put in a landscape,

n, the most beautiful building

An Art of the Open Air: Henry Moore at The New York Botanical Garden

Anita Feldman, Curator, The Henry Moore Foundation

The mounting of a major installation of Henry Moore's outdoor sculpture at The New York Botanical Garden illuminates the increasing popularity of open-air sculpture, Moore's engagement with landscape and natural forms, and his legacy as a public artist.

This exhibition follows a major display at the Royal Botanic Gardens, Kew, the first exhibition of Moore's outdoor sculpture in his native England in over 20 years. Due to logistical complications and considerations of security and expense, outdoor sculpture exhibitions are rare. Other open-air exhibitions of Moore's work have been held in Paris at the Bagatelle Gardens in 1992 and in Japan at the

fig. 1: Shelves in Bourne maquette studio, Perry Green
photo: The Henry Moore Foundation archive

Hakone Open-Air Museum in 2004. Smaller but nonetheless spectacular outdoor displays were held in Luxembourg in 1999 and in Schwäbisch Hall (Germany) and Brasilia in 2005. Although the cities of Toronto, Kansas City, and Washington, D.C., have notable collections of Moore's work, surprisingly *Moore in America: Monumental Sculpture at The New York Botanical Garden* is the first-ever exhibition in North America to concentrate solely on his outdoor sculpture: 20 works, all monumental in scale as well as in concept.[1]

The New York Botanical Garden's exhibition is not a retrospective. The Garden's installation naturally excludes a vast amount of material—it does not embrace the artist's carvings or works on paper, let alone textiles or tapestries. Yet among the sculptures displayed throughout the grounds, all of Moore's major themes are present: reclining figures, mother and child, organic forms, internal/external forms, interlocking forms, and figure as landscape. There is also an array of surface treatments, from smooth polished areas to those that are highly textured, from the bone white of fiberglass to bronze patinas of rich brown, gold, black, and vivid green.

While viewing these sculptures, it is important to keep in mind that they each started out as a clay or plaster model small enough to be held in the palm of the artist's hand and imagined any size (fig. 1). A selection of these maquettes and found objects from the artist's studio has been assembled in the Orchid Rotunda of the Library building. Moore found that using small three-dimensional maquettes enabled him to work out an idea more fully in the round than he could realize through creating numerous sketches. That he enlarged fewer than one in ten of these models is seldom acknowledged. Far from wanting to make everything big, he was very aware that there was a right size for every idea. Furthermore, he firmly believed that a work could embody a sense of monumentality without necessarily being large

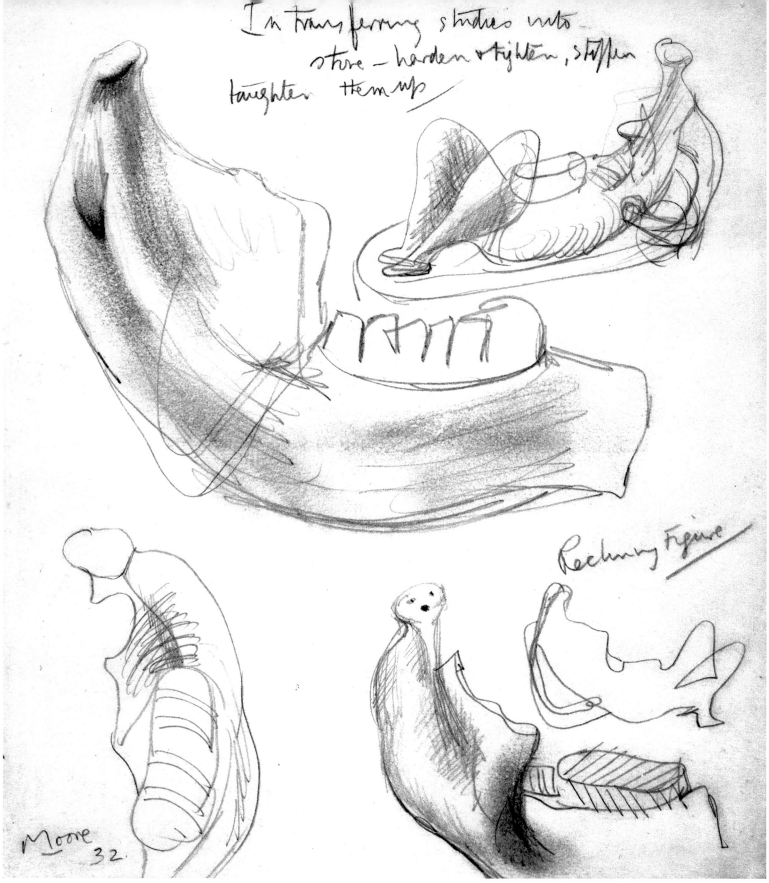

In transferring studies into
store — harden & tighten, stiffen
toughten them up

Reclining Figure

Moore
32.

fig. 2: *Ideas for Sculpture: Transformation of Bones* 1932 (HMF 941)
pencil (part rubbed and wetted) on off-white medium wove paper. 236 × 195 mm
The Henry Moore Foundation: gift of the artist, 1977
photo: The Henry Moore Foundation archive

fig. 3: *Upright Motive No. 1: Glenkiln Cross* 1955–56 in Dumfriesshire, Scotland
photo: The Henry Moore Foundation archive

in scale. Thus more representational, figurative work tended not to be enlarged over life size. Sculptures such as *Seated Woman* 1958–59 (LH 440) have a sense of weight and volume yet retain a human scale in keeping with its more contemplative and quiet mood. It benefits from a more enclosed setting such as the Garden's Rock Garden, where the rough textures of the bronze and its undulating forms are echoed in the rock surfaces and pathway along the meandering stream (p. 42).

Lending to the universal appeal of Moore's sculpture is the fact that his figures are not recognizable as individuals; they remain anonymous. With outward gazes they scan the horizon, inviting the viewer to question the nature of mankind itself in relation to its environment. Even the most seemingly abstract works are derived from the natural world, inspired by the curvature of a bone, the texture of driftwood, the internal coils of a seashell, or the smooth, pointed shapes of flints. It is the artist's lifelong exploration of natural forms that makes The New York Botanical Garden, with its rock outcroppings, native forest, and variety of foliage, so perfectly suited to his outdoor work.

A simple inscription from one of Moore's earliest notebooks anticipates his use of natural forms: "remember pebbles on the beach" is penciled on the cover of a 1926 sketchbook.[2] In his transformation drawings a few years later, and in more heavily worked compositions at the end of the decade, found objects such as stones, bones, and shells metamorphose into human figures (fig. 2). But it was not until the 1950s that Moore began to manipulate these forms in his sculpture. He first began creating works specifically for placing in

landscape when his *Standing Figure* 1950 (LH 290), *King and Queen* 1952–53 (LH 350), *Upright Motive No. 1: Glenkiln Cross* 1955–56 (LH 377), and *Two Piece Reclining Figure No. 1* 1959 (LH 457) were dramatically sited in the windswept hills of Dumfriesshire, Scotland (fig. 3). His monumental bronzes are still perceived as icons of art in landscape, not least because Moore is considered the first sculptor to have created work specifically for siting in the open air, as opposed to garden statuary, public monuments, or memorials.[3] In the traumatic aftermath of the Second World War, in which a quarter of Britain's capital city lay in ruins and rationing continued well into the subsequent decade, new approaches to public sculpture were needed. Particularly through their siting in recently rebuilt towns, Moore's family groups, reclining figures, and mother and child sculptures were imbued with a civic purpose—renewing community spirit and projecting a sense of continuity with the past as well as optimism for the future.

Twenty years later, when the majority of these works were created, Moore laid aside the social role of the artist to follow a vision that was intrinsically more personal and independent of the avant-garde. He found inspiration from nature at a time when that was not highly regarded. Critics such as Clement Greenberg who held dominion over the tide of abstract expressionism, minimalism, and conceptual art, abhorred any reference to naturalism and openly denounced Moore.[4] The changes in Moore's approach to sculpture coincided with changes in his living circumstances. From the early 1930s Moore had lived in the unparalleled artistic milieu of Hampstead, where his neighbors included many artists, architects,

fig. 4, above: Moore in his maquette studio making studies of an elephant skull
photo: Errol Jackson

fig. 5, opposite: Bourne maquette studio, Perry Green
photo: The Henry Moore Foundation archive

and intellectuals driven to England by the rise of fascism in Europe, among them Naum Gabo, Piet Mondrian, Walter Gropius, ELT Messens, and Marcel Breuer, in addition to British friends such as Julian Huxley, Barbara Hepworth, and Ben Nicholson. They would exchange ideas at the Isobar, in the Isokon building, a triumph of the new sleek modernist architecture designed by Canadian Wells Coates and run by the modern furniture industrialist Jack Pritchard, who helped many Bauhaus refugees enter Britain. All this was cut short by the outbreak of war in September 1939. Bomb damage to the Moores' house and studio in 1940, coupled with forced evacuation of their cottage in Kent, led Moore and Irina to move to the Hertfordshire countryside where they remained for the rest of their lives.

It was in Perry Green, surrounded by open fields, a medieval wood, and apple orchards, that Moore created the works inspired by nature that are so compatible with the expansive landscape of The New York Botanical Garden. At Perry Green he would unearth flint stones and animal bones from the sheep fields and draw the tangled roots of ancient trees. His "library of natural forms," which was how he referred to his maquette studio, soon filled with a variety of shapes and textures that would inform his sculptures. He observed, "I have always been very interested in landscape. (I can never read on a train—I have to look out of the window in case I miss something.) As well as landscape views and cloud formations, I find that all natural forms are a source of unending interest—tree trunks, the growth of branches from the trunk, each finding its individual air-space, the texture and variety of grasses, the shape of shells, of pebbles, etc. The whole of nature is an endless demonstration of shape and form; it always surprises me when artists try and escape from this."[5]

This aspect set Moore apart from his contemporaries and continues to be increasingly recognized and appreciated today. As recently as 1999, Belgian sculptor Ludo Bekkers wrote: "During the war and the years of occupation, I had no access whatsoever to information about what was happening in modern art elsewhere in the world. Shortly after liberation, the names and the works of artists who were opening up new horizons began to emerge…Anything that was even slightly out of line with traditional sculpture was quickly associated with [Moore's] name…So there must have been a factor in Henry Moore's work, which though considered 'modern' nevertheless had a general appeal. Could the organic origin and the reference to natural forms which are an inherent part of much of Moore's works, have been responsible?"[6]

It is not simply the organic forms, however, that make this connection between man and nature in Moore's sculpture so complete. There is also an element of time: As one approaches from a distance and walks around a sculpture, both landscape and sculpture reveal themselves gradually. Weather, light, and shifting vistas are all part of the ever-changing experience. Moore's interest in landscape was not new; he had for over 30 years been looking at the female form as a metaphor for the earth. As early as 1930 he stated: "The sculpture which moves me most is full blooded and self-supporting, fully in the round, that is, its component forms are completely realised and work as masses in opposition…it is not perfectly symmetrical, it is static and it is strong and vital, giving out

fig. 6, above: Lead maquette for *Reclining Figure* 1938 photographed by Moore outside his cottage in Kent
photo: The Henry Moore Foundation archive

fig. 7, opposite: The Woolpacks, Kinder Scout, Derbyshire, from Moore's photographic collection
photo: The Henry Moore Foundation archive

something of the energy and power of great mountains."[7] In this vein, Moore uses the versatility of bronze to open out the figure, or fragment it to take on the appearance of the land, thus completing a process of transformation.

Anyone who has ventured into the artist's studios at Perry Green realizes that there is still much to unearth, that the familiar bronzes in urban sites do not reveal the whole story. At the edge of a windswept sheep field Moore's tiny maquette studio can be found; an old wicker chair, a cane, and a turntable are positioned at its core, with cardboard boxes on the floor full of flint stones and plaster odds and ends. In a cupboard, plastic bowls contain tiny plaster heads and fragments of arms and legs. Lining all the walls are shelves crammed full of animal bones, flints, seashells, pebbles, and gnarled bits of driftwood, all intermingled with ideas for sculpture at various stages of completion. Here, the forms of man and nature become strangely indistinguishable from each other (fig. 5). There is often an unsettling ambiguity that results from natural forms carefully arranged in human form.

Viewing Moore's sculpture against the rugged hills of Yorkshire, the pastoral fields of Perry Green, or the ever-changing seasons of The New York Botanical Garden, it is immediately apparent that there is a fundamental harmony between sculpture and landscape, an elemental bond between man and nature. With Moore, however, nature is not always nurturing; there is often a tendency to sublimate the human aspect—for the figure to be fragmented and ultimately overpowered, twisted, or consumed by forces beyond human control. By emphasizing the power of nature, Moore simultaneously increases the viewer's awareness of the fragility of mankind. This is a quality we are more accustomed to associating with painting, particularly the great dramatic landscapes of the 19th century.[8] That Moore explored the power of sculpture to convey this idea is one of his unique contributions to the sculpture of the 20th century.

Photographs of rock formations (fig. 7) were used as a catalyst for some ideas, particularly the two- and three-piece reclining figures and forms separated by tense, narrow chasms such as the *Lincoln Center Reclining Figure* 1963–65 (LH 519) and *Two Piece Reclining Figure: Points* 1969 (LH 606), sited at the Botanical Garden against one of the many spectacular granite rock faces (p. 56). Local flint stones were the genesis of works such as *Reclining Mother and Child* 1975–76 (LH 649, p. 64), while seed pods can be detected as the source of *Large Totem Head* 1968 (LH 577, p. 52).

Bones provided some of the most inspired ideas for the artist. Moore had innumerable bones in his collection of found objects. These ranged from the tiniest bones of birds to fragments of animal jaws and entire skulls, including those of a black rhinoceros and an African elephant (fig. 4). Moore wrote: "By bringing the [elephant] skull very close to me and drawing various details I found so many contrasts of form and shape that I could begin to see in it great deserts and rocky landscapes, big caves in the sides of hills, great pieces of architecture, columns, and dungeons…"[9] Works such as *Working Model for Standing Figure: Knife Edge* 1961 (LH 481) manipulate the contrast between the sharp "knife-edge" of a bone and other smooth and highly textured areas. Sited in the Garden's Enid A. Haupt Conservatory, the bone white of the fiberglass provides a

'The observation of nature is a crucial part of an artist's life." —Moore, 1934

stark contrast to the dark reflecting pool and its surrounding tropical foliage (p. 44).

Large Reclining Figure 1984 (LH 192b), also in fiberglass, stands apart from the other works due to its less directly organic but rather more biomorphic forms. That is to say, the shapes have a fluid, amorphous quality more characteristic of the Surrealists and their exploration of transformation and metamorphosis. This is explained by the fact that the sculpture was enlarged from a 1938 maquette. The original sculpture in lead was a mere 33 centimeters (13 inches). Not even the wild imaginations of the Surrealists could have envisioned it being cast half a century later on such a monumental scale, although in the 1930s Moore had photographed the maquette against the sky and hills of the Kent countryside to make it appear colossal (fig. 6). An enlargement of the maquette selected by Moore and the architect I.M. Pei was created for a site in Singapore (fig. 13), and Moore positioned his artist's copy at Perry Green on top of a large hill at the end of the sheep field, where the work

benefited from being viewed in silhouette. As nearly all Moore's sculpture was intended to be experienced fully in the round, there were few other possibilities for the site. The fiberglass cast was made in order to have a version suitable for inclusion in exhibitions, its lightweight structure being more easily transportable. The white tracery is best seen against the dark foliage of the Garden or silhouetted against the sky (p. 32).

The upright motive series, of which three are included in *Moore in America*, stem from architectural rather than landscape pursuits. Although the idea for the series is frequently linked to a proposed project for the Olivetti Headquarters in Milan, the first upright motives were created in 1954 in collaboration with the architect Michael Rosenauer for the site of the new English Electric Company Headquarters on the Strand, in London.[10] The idea was to integrate sculptural elements within the concept of the building itself, rather than merely create work that would adorn an otherwise completed building. Moore's sculptures successfully unify a mixture

of organic and industrial elements into one coherent design. At the Garden, the upright motives are arranged on a series of plateaus of alternating heights to emphasize the architectural contrast of these works thrusting upward while retaining their ties to natural form (pp. 36, 38, 40).

Sculptures such as *Large Two Forms* 1966 (LH 556) take on architectural characteristics by the very fact that they are able to be entered physically. They are tough, bold forms that can hold their own against any setting. When placed in the landscape, the open forms create apertures that alter one's view of the surrounding area—vistas are ever-changing as one walks through and around the forms. They are particularly good pieces in which to observe sculptural form within the changing light and foliage throughout the seasons. At the top of Daffodil Hill, they hold one of the most expansive views of the Garden (p. 50).

There is a connection psychologically with Moore's practice of extracting found objects from the earth and returning them to the landscape as pieces of sculpture. His sculptures often convey a sense not only of timelessness but of mystery—as if we have always known them and yet they will forever retain a sense of discovery. Moore explained: "The whole of nature—bones, pebbles, shells, clouds, tree trunks, flowers—all is grist to the mill of a sculptor. It all needs to be brought in at one time. People have thought—the later Greeks, in the Hellenistic period—that the human figure was the only subject, that it ended there; a question of copying. But I believe it's a question of metamorphosis. We must relate the human figure to animals, to clouds, to the landscape—by bringing them all together. There's no difference between them all. By using them like metaphors in poetry, you give new meanings to things."[11] Archaeologist and author Jacquetta Hawkes expounded a similar connection between landscape, art, and archaeology in *A Land*, published—with illustrations by Moore—on the occasion of the 1951 Festival of Britain: "I have used the findings of the two sciences of geology and archaeology for purposes altogether unscientific. I have tried to use them evocatively, and the image I have sought to evoke is of an entity, the land of Britain, in which past, present, nature, man, and art appear all in one piece. I see modern men enjoying a unity with trilobites of a nature more deeply significant than anything at present understood in the process of biological evolution; I see a land as much affected by the creations of its poets and painters as by changes of climate and vegetation."[12]

The tradition of placing objects where they will render meaning to both the object and the chosen site is, of course, a prehistoric one. Since Moore, investigation of the relationship between man and environment continues in the work of British artists such as Ian Hamilton Finlay (1925–2006), Richard Long (b. 1945), Hamish Fulton (b. 1946), and Andy Goldsworthy (b. 1956), all of whom use found objects and local stone to convey a sense of man's intervention with the earth. Long's *A Hundred Tors in a Hundred Hours / a 114 Mile Walk on Dartmoor / Devon England* 1976 uses photography to document a journey marked by outcroppings of rock formations. The result is a photographic image remarkably similar to those Moore kept in his studio and used as inspiration for his own two- and three-piece sculptures, which in turn were sited in landscape. Found objects are also used by the American artist and anthropologist Susan Hiller (b. 1940) in investigating notions of place, culture, and memory. Hiller writes: "I have always used a concept of 'truth to material,' which accurately or not, was invariably attached to [Moore's] work when I was a student. Certainly I have used this idea against the grain and on the margins of what is defined as the practice

fig. 9, above: Anish Kapoor, *Untitled* 1997, white marble sited outside the Chiesa di San Giusto and Pinacoteca Civica in Volterra
photo: courtesy of Anish Kapoor and Lisson Gallery, London

fig. 8, opposite: *Large Square Form with Cut* 1969–71, Rio Serra marble, exhibited at the Forte di Belvedere, Florence, 1972
photo: The Henry Moore Foundation archive

fig. 10, above: David Nash,
Serpentine Vessels 1989
photo: courtesy of Annely Juda Fine Art,
London

fig. 11, opposite: *Reclining Figure* 1939, elm wood,
now in the Detroit Institute of Arts
photo: The Henry Moore Foundation archive

of sculpture. But ideas have to begin somewhere, and for me this idea started with Moore … I was intrigued to discover only recently that Moore himself did not have any doctrinaire attachment to the idea and that in terms of his work in bronze he seemed to want to free himself from any proscriptive interpretation of it."[13] Anish Kapoor (b. 1954), in his realizations of mysterious interior spaces and the void, and Rachel Whiteread (b. 1963), with her casting of interior spaces, continue the same sculptural vocabulary of internal/external forms that Moore explored throughout his career. The hollowed square white form of Kapoor's *Untitled* 1997 in white marble, placed outside the Chiesa di San Giusto and Pinacoteca Civica in Volterra, Italy, invites comparison with Moore's *Large Square Form with Cut* 1969–71 (LH 599) in Rio Serra marble sited at the Forte di Belvedere in Florence in 1972 and now in Prato, Italy (figs. 8, 9). Despite Moore's estrangement from the mainstream of the avant-garde, it would be a mistake to conclude that his work is disconnected from the art of today.

Paradoxically, the perceived distancing could in part be due to the very fact that Moore was promoted so heavily by the British Council during the Cold War. This began with a bang at the 1948 Venice Biennale, in which Moore was chosen as the sole artist to represent Britain and came home with the international prize for sculpture. In the 1952 Biennale, Moore's *Double Standing Figure* 1950 (LH 291) was exhibited at the entrance to the British Pavilion to introduce the next generation of British sculptors, whose tense angular forms revealed a post-war angst and were labeled "the geometry of fear."[14] From 1950 to 1960 the British Council organized touring exhibitions of Moore's work with a bewildering 82 venues in 20 countries.[15] That Moore's sculpture was distinctly modern yet fundamentally humanist provided a stark contrast to the bombastic realism being produced in Eastern Europe.

It could be argued that Moore's acceptance by the establishment provoked a rejection by younger artists who felt the need to be subversive in order to be noticed, culminating with the

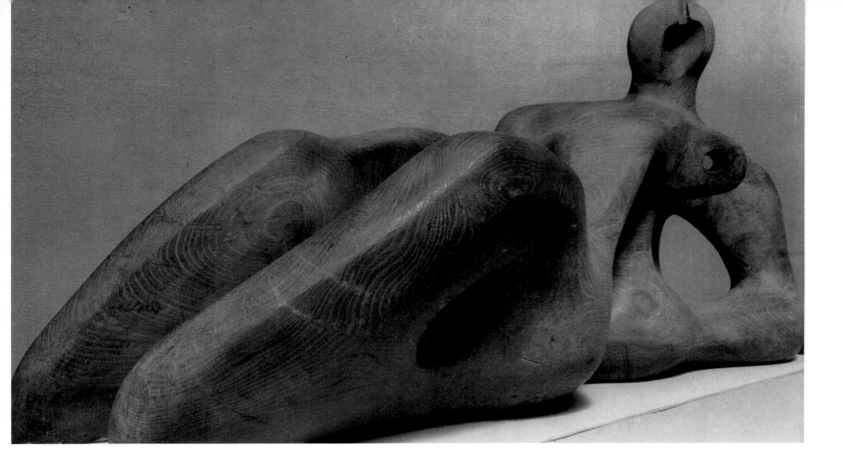

'The thing is that sculpture gains by finding a setting that suits its mood, and when that happens, there is gain for both sculpture and setting." —Moore, 1951

notoriety of later exhibitions such as the Royal Academy's *Sensation* in 1997 (which toured to the Brooklyn Museum of Art). Hiller recalled: "Moore was everywhere during my childhood, a conservative, figurative artist (we thought), a sort of official artist. He was English but his work was ubiquitous in the United States, not just in exhibitions but also in photographs in magazines and books."[16] Another response has been that of irony and includes works such as Bruce Nauman's *Seated Storage Capsule for H.M. Made of Metallic Plastic* 1966 and *Henry Moore Bound to Fail* 1967, both of which satirize Moore's interest in the mystery of interior space; Bruce McLean's *Pose Work for Plinths 3* 1971, in which he imitates the positions of Moore's reclining figures; and Howard Hodgkin's *A Henry Moore at the Bottom of the Garden* 1975–77, in which the garden is completely overgrown. Presumably the artist was too big to ignore and had to be confronted somehow.

That Moore comprehensively reworked the themes in his sculpture (although to him they were

endless and inexhaustible) also led to the sense that there was little other artists could contribute within the same sphere. Art historian David Cohen observed: "…the real reason Moore did not have followers of calibre within his own formal and thematic theory is that he developed his personal language so fully. He himself could say anything in his language, whereas anyone else who began to speak it was trapped in mimicry. This factor, more than jealousy or 'anxiety of influence' ensured that sculptors who came after him were virtually obliged to define themselves in opposition to him."[17] Hence Moore's sculpture assistants who went on to achieve fame in their own right, such as Anthony Caro and Phillip King, did so using working methods rejected by Moore, such as assemblage (creating forms through building up or welding rather than carving or reduction) and painted metal.[18] Yet Cohen himself provides compelling juxtapositions of Moore's *Three Piece Reclining Figure: Draped* 1975 (LH 655, p. 66) with Kapoor's *Mother as a Mountain* 1985 and Tony Cragg's *New Forms* 1991–92, in which the similarities between the artists' investigations of form are striking. David Nash's hollowed-out beech *Serpentine Vessels* 1989 recalls Moore's dynamic exploits in elm wood where he endeavored to open out his sculpture as far as possible within the limitations of the material, including his *Reclining Figure* 1939 (LH 210, figs. 10, 11).

The two forms in close proximity to each other, heightening the tension between them, also recall Moore's sculptures such as *Large Two Forms* 1966 (LH 556, p. 50), *Two Piece Reclining Figure: Points* 1969 (LH 606, p. 56), and *Reclining Figure: Arch Leg* 1969–70 (LH 610, p. 58). Nash invites further comparison with Moore with the creation of a work in Denmark titled *Sheep Spaces* 1993, in which two shapes with hollowed forms are situated in the landscape for sheep to lie under and brush up against as they do with Moore's *Sheep Piece* 1971–72 (LH 627) at Perry Green (fig. 12).[19]

It is now just over 20 years since Moore's death in 1986, and it will probably be another generation before his reputation can be looked at clearly with the advantage of perspective. But an exhibition such as *Moore in America*, where Moore's most powerful and monumental works are sited within landscape—as they were originally envisioned and to which they are so ideally suited—is bound to rekindle that discussion.

fig. 12: *Sheep Piece* (detail) 1971–72 at Perry Green
photo: Emily Peters

1. The last major exhibition of Moore's work in New York was held in 1983 at the Metropolitan Museum of Art in honor of the artist's 85th birthday. At the same time, Storm King Art Center in Mountainville, New York, held an exhibition with 7 outdoor sculptures and 11 indoor pieces. The same year, 15 outdoor works from a single private collection were displayed at Blue Hill Plaza in Pearl River, New York, immediately prior to the collection's dispersal. The most recent major retrospective in the United States was held in 2001–02 at the Dallas Museum of Art, the Fine Arts Museums of San Francisco Legion of Honor, and the National Gallery of Art in Washington, D.C.

2. *Notebook No. 6* 1926, The Henry Moore Foundation: gift of the artist, 1977.

3. A possible exception is Brancusi's 1938 *Endless Column* in Targu-Jiu, Romania.

4. See Clement Greenberg, "Arrogant Purpose," *Collected Essays and Criticism*, vol. 2, 1944–49, University of Chicago Press, Chicago 1986, pp. 126–7.

5. *Henry Moore: Energie im Raum*, Bruckmann, Munich 1973, p. 19.

6. Ludo Bekkers, "Henry Moore: A Review," *Henry Moore Sculpturen/Tekeningen*, Openluchtmuseum voor Beelhouwkunst Middelheim, Museum van Hedendaagse Kunst, Antwerp 1999, p. 9.

7. Henry Moore "A View of Sculpture," originally published as "Contemporary English Sculptors: Henry Moore," *Architectural Association Journal*, May 1930, p. 408; reprinted in Alan Wilkinson, *Henry Moore: Writings and Conversations*, Ashgate, Aldershot 2002, p. 188.

8. For example, the landscapes of Joseph Mallord Turner (1775–1851), John Martin (1789–1854), and James Ward (1769–1859), in which figures or animals are overwhelmed by the forces of nature.

9. Moore's typed notes from 1970 referring to his studies of an elephant skull. The Henry Moore Foundation archive; published in Wilkinson, op.cit., pp. 297–8.

10. The proposed structure was never built as Rosenauer lost the commission to Gordon Tate. A similar concept was carried out for the site of the Time-Life Building on Bond Street also designed by Rosenauer with a pierced screen by Moore in Portland stone.

11. Carlton Lake, "Henry Moore's World," *Atlantic Monthly*, Boston, January 1962, p. 42; cited in Wilkinson, op.cit., p. 222.

12. Jacquetta Hawkes, preface to *A Land*, Cresset Press Ltd, London 1951.

13. Susan Hiller, "Truth and Truth to Material: Reflecting on the Sculptural Legacy of Henry Moore," *Henry Moore: Critical Essays,* The Henry Moore Institute, Ashgate, Aldershot 2003, pp. 67–8. "Truth to material'" was an aesthetic approach to sculpture that Moore adhered to in his pre-war carvings in which the shape and form of a sculpture was informed by the material itself—the block of stone or grain of wood. Eventually Moore found the idea too limiting and worked in bronze largely to allow more freedom in the invention of forms.

14. Artists included Robert Adams, Kenneth Armitage, Reg Butler, Lynn Chadwick, Geoffrey Clarke, Bernard Meadows, Eduardo Paolozzi, and William Turnbull. The name for the group was coined by Herbert Read.

fig. 13: Moore with his assistant Malcolm Woodward in 1983, during the enlargement of *Large Reclining Figure*
photo: Errol Jackson

15. Belgium, France, Holland, Germany, Switzerland, Greece, Mexico, Austria, Sweden, Norway, Denmark, Finland, Yugoslavia, Czechoslovakia, Canada, New Zealand, South Africa, Japan, Portugal, and Spain.

16. Hiller, op.cit.

17. David Cohen, "Who's Afraid of Henry Moore?" *Henry Moore: Sculpting the 20th Century*, Dallas Museum of Art and Yale University Press, New Haven and London 2001, p. 266.

18. Even Moore's bronzes, which are necessarily welded together as part of the casting process, began as models in plaster that were cut back or carved to achieve the desired form.

19. See Julian Andrews, *The Sculpture of David Nash*, Lund Humphries, London 1996, p. 122.

MOORE
IN AMERICA

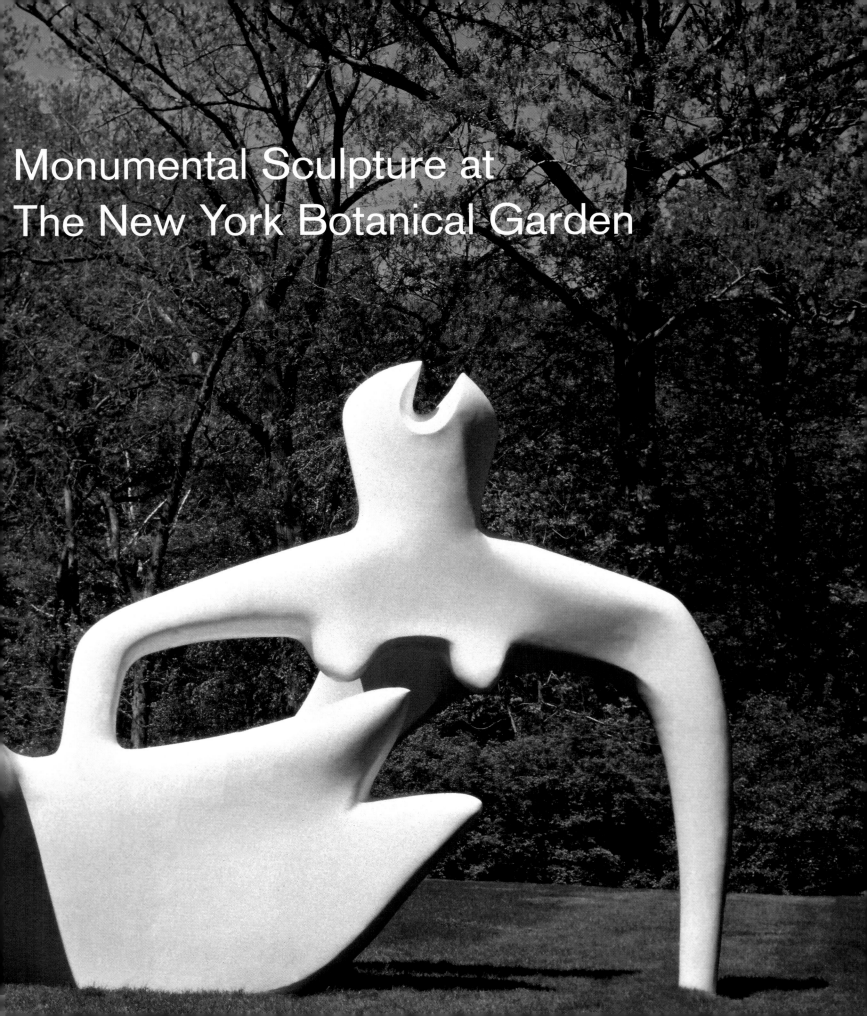

Monumental Sculpture at
The New York Botanical Garden

At the Henry Moore Foundation in Perry Green, Hertfordshire, a bronze cast of *Large Reclining Figure* lies atop a hillock, surveying the estate below. The figure has a striking impact: She appears to be perched, her open slender body leaning on the grass. The shape, though pointed, has a delicate, smooth outline. The simple abstract head appears open, looking skyward, leaving the question of its expression to the viewer's imagination. The frontal aspect of the figure shifts, allowing penetration and views through the work.

As well as the cast in Perry Green, a bronze with a gold patina stands alongside the Overseas Chinese Bank Headquarters in Singapore. The building was designed by the Chinese-born American architect I.M. Pei, and standing 52 stories high, it was on completion in 1976 the tallest building in the Far East. This commission was the fourth and final collaboration between Moore and Pei, who engineered a plaza within the complex specifically for the monumental sculpture.

The work seen at the Garden was cast from a polystyrene and plaster enlargement of a small lead maquette for *Reclining Figure* 1938 (see p. 20). Moore increasingly found that carving in stone and wood had its limitations, and he wanted to preserve the integrity of the material he utilized. Bronze casting permitted him to delve into the form, and the sculptures increasingly opened out, enabling the exploration of internal space within the figure.

Moore did not use fiberglass often, although it had certain advantages due to its lightweight nature. Fiberglass does not have the durability of bronze or the range of finish and color, but it enables large-scale works to be produced and transported easily.

1984
LH 192b
fiberglass
cast: Edward Lawrence Studios, Midhurst
length: 900 cm approx. (29.5 ft.)
The Henry Moore Foundation: acquired 1987
Location: Benenson Ornamental Conifers

Mother and Child

1949
LH 269b
bronze edition of 1 + 1
cast: Fiorini, London
height: 81 cm (2.6 ft.)
The Henry Moore Foundation:
gift of the artist, 1977
Location: Everett Children's Adventure Garden

"I suppose the favourite form motives of any individual artist are an inescapable part of his make-up—(and [if I] could give a psychological explanation) I might be able to give some sort of convincing reason for my liking of the mother and child theme from knowledge of my own history." —Moore, 1941

Moore created this work as part of a larger family group on which he worked from 1945 to 1948. For this composition, however, he focused on the head and shoulders of the mother with the child in her arms. The mother's arms are intertwined with her child in an all-encompassing embrace. This is not a natural cradling position but more of a presentation, a reaching out toward the viewer rather than a private family moment.

The division of the solid mass into two forms is another enduring aspect of Moore's work. The connection between the pieces is inferred on this occasion through the relationship between mother and child. This theme resurfaced again and again in Moore's work, at times explicitly and at others implicitly as with his internal/external forms. As a subject in both human and compositional terms, it provided him with endless possibilities.

1955–56
LH 383
bronze edition of 7 + 1
cast: The Art Bronze Foundry, London
height: 213.5 cm (7 ft.)
signature: stamped *Moore*, [0/7]
The Henry Moore Foundation:
gift of the artist, 1977
Location: Benenson Ornamental Conifers

Upright Motive No. 7

1955–56
LH 386
bronze edition of 5 + 1
cast: H.H. Martyn, Cheltenham
height: 320 cm (10.4 ft.)
The Henry Moore Foundation:
gift of the artist, 1977
Location: Benenson Ornamental Conifers

Upright Motive No. 8

1955–56
LH 388
bronze edition of 7 + 1
cast: Corinthian, London
height: 198 cm (6.4 ft.)
The Henry Moore Foundation:
gift of the artist, 1979
Location: Benenson Ornamental Conifers

"Sculpture is like a journey. You have a different view as you return. The three-dimensional world is full of surprises in a way that a two-dimensional world could never be." —Moore, 1962

The idea of a series of upright motives began while Moore was working with Michael Rosenauer on a design for the English Electric Company Headquarters in London in 1954. Moore produced six upright motive maquettes and two maquettes for corner sculptures as integral parts of Rosenauer's project. Although the design didn't win the commission, these maquettes became the impetus for the upright motives series.

The theme resurfaced in the same year when Moore was commissioned to produce a sculpture for a square in the new Olivetti building in Milan. He felt that the space required a vertical work to offset the primarily horizontal design of the building. He began work on an upright composition, and several maquettes were made. The project was never realized, as Moore discovered that the area around the work would be used as a car park.

Moore worked with architects throughout his career: Rosenauer, Charles Holden, Gordon Bunshaft, and I.M. Pei among others. Moore considered, however, that in general his works' full potential was best realized within a natural landscape, thus making an architectural background a considerable challenge for him.

These motives, three of which are included in the exhibition at The New York Botanical Garden, bring to mind Native American totem poles—an association acknowledged by Moore himself. In speaking of *Upright Motive No. 8,* Moore referred to a Jamaican wood carving of a bird man, which he saw in the British Museum. The sentry-like pieces are confident and solid; their truncated forms have nooks and crannies, deep grooves, and intriguing orifices. The motives seem to be life-size—though in reality they are twice as big—and appear ambiguously figurative.

Seated Woman

1958–59
LH 440
bronze edition of 6 + 1
cast: Hermann Noack, Berlin 1975
height: 211 cm (6.9 ft.)
signature: stamped *Moore 0/6*
The Henry Moore Foundation: acquired 1987
Location: Rock Garden

Working Model for Standing Figure: Knife Edge

1961
LH 481
fiberglass edition of 0 + 2
cast: Norman and Raymond, London
height: 162.5 cm (5.3 ft.)
The Henry Moore Foundation:
gift of the artist, 1977
Location: Enid A. Haupt Conservatory

"In this figure the thin neck and head, by contrast with the width and bulk of the body, give more monumentality to the work … in walking round this sculpture the width and flatness from the front gradually change through the three quarter views into the thin sharp edges of the side views, and then back again to the width seen from the back …" —Moore, 1965

Moore relied on a variety of natural sources for his ideas for sculpture, such as bones, stones, pebbles, shells, and wood. These he collected over the years and kept in his maquette studio, where many were placed unsystematically on a series of shelves alongside small sculptural works. They are still on display at the Henry Moore Foundation in Hertfordshire, England.

This delicate, graceful, figurative form originated from a segment of bone, which Moore upended and to which he added a small head. The surface texture is extremely varied, with smooth planes and pitted areas increasing the tonality of the exterior. This fiberglass cast was colored with a powdered material that Moore often used to give plaster and fiberglass pieces tone and depth of shade.

There are similarities between this work and the elegant *Nike of Samothrace* from Ancient Greece, now in the Louvre. *Winged Figure* and *Standing Figure Bone* were two other considered titles, but the sharp points and edges prompted the final decision on its name. The angular corners where the butcher's knife sheared the bone into pieces are in stark contrast to the gentle curve of the neck and head and outstretched arms.

Locking Piece

_____

1963–64
LH 515
bronze edition of 3 + 1
cast: Hermann Noack, Berlin
height: 290 cm (9.5 ft.)
The Henry Moore Foundation:
acquired 1987
Location: outside Rock Garden

"…I was playing with a couple of pebbles…[and I found that]…they got locked together and I couldn't get them undone and I wondered how they got into that position and it was like a clenched fist…This gave one the idea of making two forms which would do that and later I called it *Locking Piece* because they lock together." —Moore, ca. 1980

Standing in front of these two intertwined bronze forms, one wants to solve the puzzle. Do the pieces come apart? The echo of the pebbles that stimulated the artist is still clear. The two forms curve around each other and appear inextricably knotted together. Intrigued by the shapes, exploring the different points of contact, as observers we recognize the grinding weight of the upper form pressing down on its lower half.

Moore was fascinated by found objects such as flint stones, driftwood, and animal bones. The sculptures on display at The New York Botanical Garden are distinguished by their monumentality, but their origin was often more intimate. So, too, was Moore's design method. When he returned to sculpting after the war, Moore began making small models with a view to developing a form worthy of enlargement. He found that this technique enabled him to see the work from all angles, saving him from having to execute countless drawings. From 1929 Moore lived and worked in Hampstead, London, with his wife, Irina, but when their home suffered irreparable bomb damage during the Blitz in 1940, the couple decided to move to the relative tranquility of the Hertfordshire countryside. One advantage of this relocation was the predominance of animal bones and flint stones in the surrounding fields of their new home.

Over the years Moore built up an enormous collection of these natural forms, which formed the basis of many small maquettes. A selection of the most successful were enlarged—sometimes on a grand scale, as we see in the works exhibited at the Garden.

Knife Edge Two Piece

1962–65
LH 516
bronze edition of 3 + 1
cast: Hermann Noack, Berlin
length: 366 cm (12 ft.)
signature: stamped *Moore 0/3*
The Henry Moore Foundation:
gift of the artist, 1977
Location: Garden Way near Main Tram Stop

Moore grew up in Castleford, an industrial town in the north of England.
Within only a few miles of his home were the hills and dales of Yorkshire, an area
renowned for its majestic scenery. On family expeditions he would explore the
rugged countryside strewn with rocks and boulders—monumental organic forms
peppering the landscape.

There are traces of these childhood experiences within Moore's full-scale sculptures. This piece outlines the harmony of the solid mass of the bronze and its
negative space. Both are crucial to the enormity and weight of the work; the
divide gives us a peek through it, framing a slice of its surroundings, inviting us
to explore both the piece itself and the effect it has on its environs. The two
forms are similar in shape but indicate the organic asymmetry characteristic of
Moore's work.

This work embodies solidity: the organic, wedge-like forms slice through the sky.
There is tension between the two segments as they stretch upward side by side. The
space separating them is a ravine, cutting a swathe through to the view behind.

Throughout his career Moore relied on a handful of foundries to cast his work.
The large-scale bronzes were produced at Morris Singer in Basingstoke, England,
or, as in the case of this work, Hermann Noack in Berlin. Other foundries he
used included three London companies, Galizia, Fiorini, and the Art Bronze
Foundry, as well as Susse Fondeur in Paris.

This work is familiar to the United Kingdom, as a cast stands in Parliament
Square in London, and often forms the backdrop for televised interviews. A
larger but reversed version, *Mirror Knife Edge* 1977 (LH 714), was made for the
entrance to the east wing of the National Gallery of Art, Washington, D.C.,
designed by I.M. Pei.

Large Two Forms

1966
LH 556
bronze edition of 4 + 1
cast: Hermann Noack, Berlin
length: 610 cm (20 ft.)
signature: stamped *Moore 0/4*
The Henry Moore Foundation: acquired 1992
Location: Daffodil Hill

Large Two Forms has enormous impact, viewed both at close quarters and from a distance. It is a work that needs to be explored thoroughly in the round. Moore designed the sculpture to be sited directly on the ground, making it part of the landscape, like rocks deposited by glacial drift. The two enormous bronze elements are gently curved, sympathetically rising and falling with each other's contours. As with many of the sculptures on display at The New York Botanical Garden, the space between the two forms is critical to the monumentality of the piece. The gap allows passage through the work, enabling the viewer not only to explore the two forms from within, but also to experience the physical presence of the sculpture.

Large Two Forms demonstrates one of the central themes of Moore's work: the simplicity of organic mass. As one moves around the work, the importance of the holes becomes apparent: Looking through them the viewer sees not only the landscape but a portion of the other form. The surface is smooth, with a rich green patina that echoes the hues of the natural setting; the variations within the surface color create depth and shade.

A hidden component of the sculpture is crucial to its stability. Each piece has a steel frame below ground, supporting the mass of bronze. There is a footprint for positioning this work, and when moved it has to be dug out of the ground and lifted with a heavy-duty crane. Each new site must be prepared carefully, and footings are built to ensure that the work sits on a solid foundation.

Another cast of this work was selected for the forecourt of the former German Federal Chancellery in Bonn. At the unveiling of the piece in September 1979, Helmut Schmidt, then Chancellor of a divided country, exclaimed that it symbolized "human solidarity and an expression of humanity."

Large Totem Head

1968
LH 577
bronze edition of 8 + 1
cast: Hermann Noack, Berlin
height: 244 cm (8 ft.)
signature: stamped *Moore 0/8*
The Henry Moore Foundation: acquired 1987
Location: Snuff Mill Road at Azalea Way

Oval with Points

1968–70
LH 596
bronze edition of 6 + 1
cast: Morris Singer, Basingstoke
height: 332 cm (10.8 ft.)
signature: stamped *Moore 0/6*
The Henry Moore Foundation:
gift of the artist, 1977
Location: Garden Way near Main Tram Stop

Two Piece Reclining Figure: Points

1969
LH 606
bronze edition of 7 + 1
cast: Hermann Noack, Berlin
length: 365 cm (11.9 ft.)
signature: stamped *Moore 0/7*
The Henry Moore Foundation:
gift of the artist, 1977
Location: near Daffodil Hill

Growing up in an industrial town in the north of England close to the Yorkshire hills and pictur-esque valleys may have formed the basis of Moore's interest in organic form and structure. Although he did work with architects throughout his career and many of his works are sited in urban areas, Moore preferred a natural surrounding for his sculpture, making The New York Botanical Garden an ideal backdrop.

Intertwined with his fascination in the human form, the natural formation of found objects — rocks, bones, shells, and driftwood — often became a starting point for sculpture. Moore worked with small three-dimensional maquettes in plaster or clay, observing them from every angle. A selection of these would be scaled up to working models, and some were then enlarged to life-size.

This development never strayed far from the original inspiration. *Two Piece Reclining Figure: Points* 1969 (LH 606) and *Seated Woman* 1958–59 (LH 440, p. 42) are both rock and female figure. *Two Piece Reclining Figure: Points* explores the human figure as landscape. The body is divided into two and metamorphosed into stark rocky outcrops. The abstraction still retains female qualities, however; her face is clearly visible, as is a hint of breast. The space between the points is carefully considered, creating tension as the two parts are separated but reach toward each other in perpetuity.

Reclining Figure: Arch Leg

1969–70
LH 610
bronze edition of 6 + 1
cast: Hermann Noack, Berlin
length: 442 cm (14.5 ft.)
The Henry Moore Foundation: acquired 1987
Location: outside Peggy Rockefeller Rose Garden

Hill Arches

1973
LH 636
bronze edition of 3 + 1
cast: Hermann Noack, Berlin
length: 550 cm (18 ft.)
signature: stamped *Moore 0/3*
The Henry Moore Foundation:
gift of the artist, 1977
Location: Library building lawn

Goslar Warrior

1973–74
LH 641
bronze edition of 7 + 1
cast: Hermann Noack, Berlin
length: 300 cm (9.8 ft.)
signature: stamped *Moore 0/7*
The Henry Moore Foundation:
gift of the artist, 1977
Location: Leon Levy Visitor Center

Reclining Mother and Child

1975–76
LH 649
bronze edition of 7 + 1
cast: Hermann Noack, Berlin
length: 213 cm (6.9 ft.)
signature: stamped *Moore 0/7*
The Henry Moore Foundation: acquired 1986
Location: Peggy Rockefeller Rose Garden

Three Piece Reclining Figure: Draped

1975
LH 655
bronze edition of 7 + 1
cast: Morris Singer, Basingstoke
length: 474 cm (15.5 ft.)
signature: stamped *Moore 0/7*
The Henry Moore Foundation: acquired 1987
Location: Benenson Ornamental Conifers

Reclining Figure: Angles

1979
LH 675
bronze edition of 9 + 1
cast: Hermann Noack, Berlin
length: 218 cm (7.1 ft.)
signature: stamped *Moore 0/9*
The Henry Moore Foundation: acquired 1986
Location: Azalea Way

Draped Reclining Mother and Baby

1983
LH 822
bronze edition of 9 + 1
cast: Morris Singer, Basingstoke
length: 265.5 cm (8.7 ft.)
signature: stamped *Moore 0/9*
The Henry Moore Foundation: acquired 1986
Location: Native Plant Garden

The 'Mother and child' idea is one of my two or three obsessions, one of my inexhaustible subjects ... But the subject itself is eternal and unending, with so many sculptural possibilities in it—a small form in relation to a big form protecting the small one, and so on. It is such a rich subject, both humanly and compositionally, that I will always go on using it." —Moore, 1979

Draped Reclining Mother and Baby was cast in 1983 as Moore was nearing the end of his life. The work is an amalgamation of three themes that appeared throughout his career: the reclining figure, mother and child, and the internal/external.

The division of the solid mass into two forms is another enduring aspect of Moore's work. The connection investigated between the pieces is inferred on this occasion through the relationship between mother and child.

The body of the mother has an undulating form that reflects an exaggerated landscape: a shallow cave carved in the side of a rock through years of erosion. One enveloping arm shields her child, creating a haven, a nestling place. The bond between parent and child in *Draped Reclining Mother and Baby* is reiterated in their positions. The curvaceous mother lounges; she is grounded, suggesting permanence and stability. She rests with her ward in her arms, the child gazing upward to his mother, while she looks confidently out in front toward the viewer. The child has a fully formed figurative outline, an independent physical form rather than being a continuation of his mother's mass.

Moore's lifelong study of this favorite subject had been wide-ranging and tireless, and he once commented that he could turn "every little scribble, blot, or smudge" into a mother and child.[1]

[1] *Henry Moore*, John Hedgecoe, Nelson, London 1968, p. 61

Installation of *Moore in America*

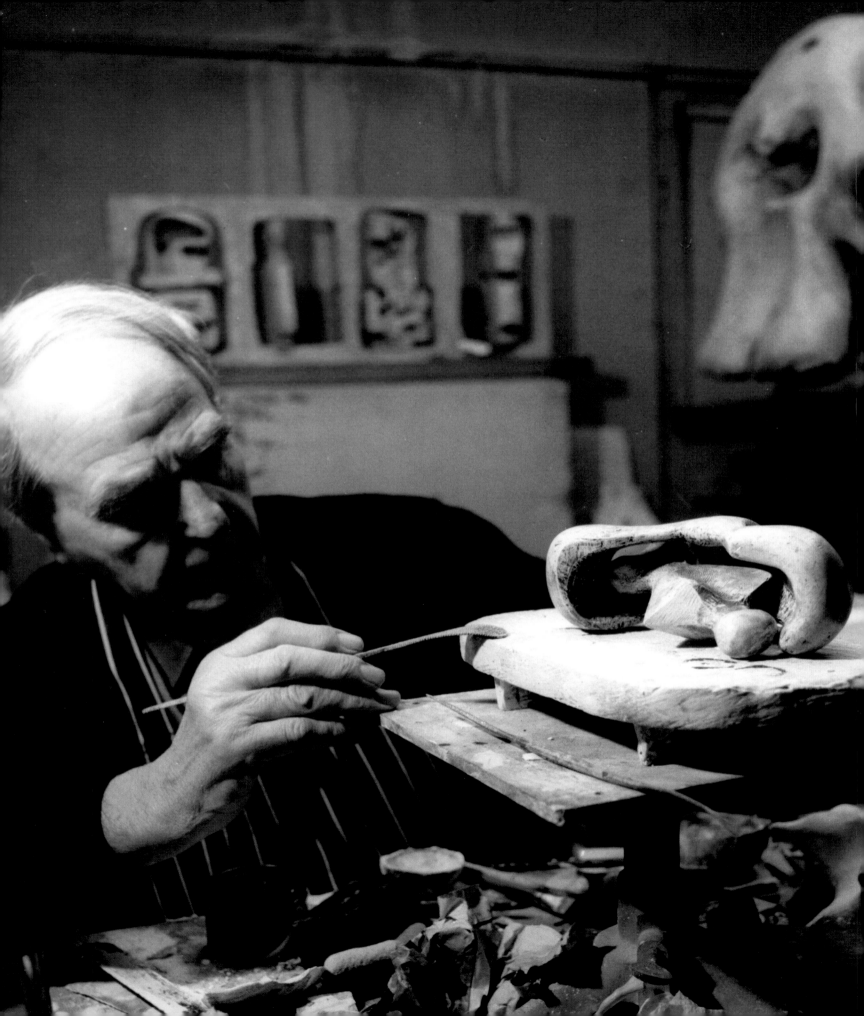

Materials and Tools Used by Moore

stone

African green stone
African wonderstone
alabaster
    Cumberland alabaster
    veined alabaster
    white alabaster
Ancaster stone
    blue Ancaster stone
anhydrite stone
bathstone
Burgundy stone
Corsehill stone
Corsham stone
Darley Dale stone
granite
    black granite
green gneiss
green soapstone
green stone
Hadene stone
Ham Hill stone
Hopton Wood stone
Hornton stone
    blue Hornton stone
    brown Hornton stone
    green Hornton stone

ironstone
Mansfield stone
marble
    Armenian marble
    black marble
    black Abyssinian marble
    bird's-eye marble
    Carrara marble
    Rio Serra marble
    Rosa Aurora marble
    travertine marble
    red travertine marble
    Roman travertine marble
    verdi di Prato
    white marble
    white crystalline marble
Portland stone
rock salt
serpentine
    black serpentine
    green serpentine
slate
stalactite
stone
styrian jade

wood

African wood
beech wood
boxwood
cherry wood
ebony
elm wood
lignum vitae
oak
pynkado wood
sycamore wood
walnut wood
yew wood

metal

bronze
cast iron
gold
lead
silver

other materials

bone
brick
clay (white)
concrete
elastic
fiberglass
fishing line
flint
gesso
hessian
paint
plaster
plasticine
polystyrene
polyurethane foam
porcelain
resin
string
terra-cotta
wax
wire (brass)

for stone

banker turntable
bouchard hammer
carborundum stone
chisel
claw
flat
lump hammer
pitcher
point
rasp
riffler
stone axe
wet and dry sandpaper

for wood

chainsaw
chisel
cross-cut saw
gouge
mallet
dummy mallet
rasp
sandpaper
surform

for clay

armature wire (aluminum)
kidney scraper
modeling stand
wooden modeling tools

for plaster

caliper
cheese grater
chisel
dentist's tools
enlarging frame
file
hand axe
mallet
metal modeling tools
rasp
riffler
sandpaper
saw
spatula
surform
tape measure
trowel
walnut crystals

for polystyrene

hot wire
marker pen
sandpaper
saw
wire brush

Moore in his studio working on *Maquette for
Reclining Connected Forms* 1968
photo: Ashieri

Chronology of Moore's Life and Work

1917
Private Moore shortly after he joined the army at age 19
photo: The Henry Moore Foundation archive

1920
Moore (center) with fellow drawing exam students at Leeds School of Art
photo: The Henry Moore Foundation archive

1928–29
Moore carving *West Wind* 1928–29 for the façade of the London Underground headquarters at St. James's Park station
photo: The Henry Moore Foundation archive

July 30, 1898

Henry Spencer Moore is born, the seventh of eight children, in Castleford, Yorkshire, where his father is a coal miner.

1917

Enlists in the Civil Service Rifles, 15th London Regiment and serves in First World War; is gassed at the Battle of Cambrai and returns to England to convalesce.

1919–20

Attends Leeds School of Art, where a sculpture department is set up with Moore as the sole student.

1921

Wins a scholarship to study sculpture at the Royal College of Art, London. Begins frequent visits to the British Museum where he fills sketchbooks with studies of sculpture from around the world.

1922

Develops his interest in direct carving and in the work of Henri Gaudier-Brzeska and Constantin Brancusi. Visits Paris, where he is deeply impressed by Paul Cézanne's paintings in the Auguste Pellerin collection. His family moves to Norfolk, where during vacations Moore makes his first carvings.

1924

Takes part in his first group exhibition at the Redfern Gallery, London. Appointed instructor of the sculpture department at the Royal College of Art.

1925

Traveling scholarship takes him, via Paris, to Rome, Florence, Pisa, Siena, Assisi, Padua, Ravenna, and Venice.

1928

His first one-man exhibition is held at the Warren Gallery, London; drawings bought by Jacob Epstein and Augustus John. Meets Irina Radetsky, a painting student at the Royal College.

1929

Moore and Irina are married; they move to Hampstead, which becomes a center for artists, architects, and writers in the 1930s, including Naum Gabo, Piet Mondrian, Walter Gropius, Marcel Breuer, László Moholy-Nagy, Ben Nicholson, and Barbara Hepworth. Carves the Hornton stone *Reclining Figure* (LH 59) now in Leeds City Art Gallery, completes *West Wind* (LH 58), a relief in Portland stone on the headquarters of the London Underground, St. James's Park.

1930

Exhibits with the Young Painters' Society and the London Group; chosen (with Epstein and John Skeaping) to represent Britain at the Venice Biennial.

1931

Resigns from his teaching post at the Royal College of Art. Following a one-man exhibition at the Leicester Galleries, London, his first work is sold abroad, to a museum in Hamburg. Becomes first head of sculpture in new department at Chelsea School of Art. Buys a cottage in Kent where he can carve in the open air.

1932

Completes 20 carvings in wood and stone, including *Mother and Child* (LH 121), now in the Sainsbury Centre for Visual Arts (University of East Anglia), Norwich, England.

1933

Second exhibition at the Leicester Galleries, London. Chosen to become a member of Unit One, a group of avant-garde artists. In Paris he meets Alberto Giacometti, Ossip Zadkine, and Jacques Lipchitz.

1934

Travels with Irina and friends to see prehistoric cave paintings in Altamira, Spain, and Les Eyzies-de-Tayac, France. In Spain, Moore also visits Barcelona, Madrid, and Toledo. The first monograph on his work, by Herbert Read, is published. Moore's carving *Two Forms* (LH 153) in pynkado wood is acquired by the Museum of Modern Art in New York.

1935

Buys a larger cottage with land near Canterbury, Kent, where he makes many carvings in the open air. As the size of his carvings increases, he makes use of small preliminary models, known as *maquettes*.

1936

Finishes his first major elmwood carving, *Reclining Figure* (LH 175), now in Wakefield Art Gallery, England. Serves on the Organizing Committee of the *International Surrealist Exhibition* at the New Burlington Galleries, London, in which he also takes part. Signs the Surrealist manifesto.

1937

Begins a series of stringed figures inspired by mathematical models in the Science Museum, London. Accompanies Roland Penrose to Paris, and with Giacometti, Paul Eluard, André Breton, and Max Ernst, visits Picasso in his studio to see *Guernica* in progress.

1938

Attempts to visit Spain as part of a delegation of writers and artists opposing Fascism but is refused permission to travel by the British government. His work is represented at the *International Exhibition of Abstract Art* at the Stedelijk Museum, Amsterdam. Carves *Recumbent Figure* (LH 184), now in Tate Britain, for the garden of architect Serge Chermayeff.

1939

On the outbreak of war he is forced to give up his post, when Chelsea School of Art closes, as well as his cottage in Kent, as the area is evacuated due to threat of invasion. Draws *September 3rd 1939* (HMF 1551) of bathers near the Dover cliffs the day war is declared. Produces his first lithograph, *Spanish Prisoner* (CGM 3), intended to be sold in aid of Spanish prisoners of war.

1940

He and Irina move to Perry Green, Hertfordshire, when their London home and studio is damaged during an air raid. Begins Shelter Drawings of figures in the London Underground during the Blitz.

1942

Commissioned by the War Artists' Advisory Committee to make a series of drawings of coal miners at Wheldale Colliery, near Castleford, the mine in which his father had worked.

1944

Madonna and Child (LH 226) is installed in St. Matthew's Church, Northampton, England.

1932
Mother and Child 1932 in the artist's studio, 11a Parkhill Road, Hampstead, now in the Robert and Lisa Sainsbury Collection, University of East Anglia, Norwich
photo: The Henry Moore Foundation archive

1948–49
Moore outside his studio with the plaster of *Family Group* 1948–49
photo: The Henry Moore Foundation archive

1951
Moore with *Reclining Figure: Festival* 1951
photo: The Henry Moore Foundation archive

1952
Moore working on one of the four main components of the screen for Michael Rosenauer's Time-Life Building, Perry Green
photo: The Henry Moore Foundation archive

1959
Moore carving *Reclining Figure* 1959–64 in Perry Green
photo: The Henry Moore Foundation archive

1946
Birth of the Moores' only child, Mary. Moore's first retrospective held at the Museum of Modern Art, New York.

1948
Represents Britain at the XXIV Venice Biennial, where he is awarded the International Prize for Sculpture. Begins work on *Family Group* (LH 269) for a school in Stevenage, England — perhaps surprisingly, this and *Harlow Family Group* 1955 (LH 364) would be the only family group sculptures he would develop beyond the maquette stage.

1950
Moore refuses the offer of a knighthood.

1951
Moore's first retrospective at the Tate Gallery; *Reclining Figure: Festival* (LH 293) is exhibited on the South Bank during the Festival of Britain. He tours Greece on the occasion of his exhibition in Athens.

1952
A period of intense sculptural activity includes a series of standing figures, internal/external forms, and reliefs; work begins on two sculptures for the Time-Life Building in Bond Street, London, and *King and Queen* (LH 350); all three completed the following year.

1953
Moore attends the second São Paulo Biennial, where he is awarded the International Sculpture Prize; afterward he tours Brazil and Mexico.

1955
Makes a series of *Upright Motives* (LH 376-392a). Appointed Member of the Order of the Companions of Honour; made a Trustee of the National Gallery, London (1955–74).

1956
Receives a sculpture commission for Marcel Breuer's UNESCO headquarters in Paris.

1958
Appointed Chairman of the Auschwitz Memorial Committee.

1959
Begins large elmwood *Reclining Figure* (LH 452) and completes the bronze *Two Piece Reclining Figure No. 1* (LH 457) the first in a series of sculptures that fragment the figure to resemble landscape.

1965
Completes *Knife Edge Two Piece* (LH 516), a cast of which is sited outside the Houses of Parliament in London. Visits New York for the installation of *Reclining Figure* (LH 519) at Lincoln Center. Buys a house in Forte dei Marmi, Italy, where he and his family spend subsequent summer holidays.

1967
Attends the unveiling of *Nuclear Energy* (LH 526) on the University of Chicago campus. Is named Honorary Doctor, Royal College of Art, London, and Fellow of the British Academy.

1968
A retrospective at the Tate Gallery, London, marks Moore's 70th birthday; at an exhibition at the Rijksmuseum Kröller-Müller in the Netherlands, he receives the Erasmus Prize. Awarded the Einstein Prize by Yeshiva University, New York. Begins work on monumental bronze *Three Piece Sculpture: Vertebrae* (LH 580).

1972

A spectacular retrospective exhibition is held at the Forte di Belvedere, Florence; Moore attends the opening by Princess Margaret, and later presents a cast of *Warrior with Shield* (LH 360) to the city of Florence. Begins drawing the *Sheep Sketchbook*, which in turn leads to an album of sheep etchings.

1974

Inauguration of the Henry Moore Sculpture Centre at the Art Gallery of Ontario, Toronto, to which Moore donates 101 sculptures, 57 drawings, and an almost complete collection of lithographs and etchings.

1977

Inauguration of the Henry Moore Foundation. Exhibition at the Orangerie des Tuileries, Paris.

1978

Moore's 80th birthday is marked by exhibitions at the Tate Gallery and Serpentine Gallery in London, and the City Art Gallery, Bradford, England. He makes a gift of 36 sculptures to the Tate. *Mirror: Knife Edge* (LH 714) installed at the National Gallery of Art, Washington, D.C.

1979

Now suffering from arthritis in his hands and finding sculpting difficult, Moore devotes more time to drawing and graphic work; makes series of etchings and lithographs of trees and hands.

1980

Moore's tapestries are exhibited at the Victoria and Albert Museum, London. A large marble version of *The Arch* (LH 503c) is donated to the Department of the Environment (now Royal Parks) for Kensington Gardens. Moore is awarded the Grand Cross of the Order of Merit of the Federal Republic of Germany. Despite declining health, he completes 350 drawings.

1982

The Henry Moore Sculpture Gallery and Centre for the Study of Sculpture (now the Henry Moore Institute) is opened by Queen Elizabeth as an extension to Leeds City Art Gallery.

1984

Named *Commandeur de l'Ordre National de la Légion d'Honneur* when French President Mitterrand visits him at Perry Green. A touring exhibition of war drawings opens at the Nationalgalerie in East Berlin.

1985

Moore creates *Large Figure in a Shelter* (LH 652c) for Guernica.

August 31, 1986

Moore dies at Perry Green, aged 88. A Service of Thanksgiving for his life and work is held on November 18 in Westminster Abbey, London.

1968–69
Moore with Hermann Noack at the foundry in Berlin discussing the progress of *Three Piece Sculpture: Vertebrae* 1968–69
photo: The Henry Moore Foundation archive

1978
From left, Phillip King, Anthony Caro, and Moore sharing a joke at the opening of Moore's 80th birthday exhibition at Bradford, England
photo: Errol Jackson

Selected Publications

Bibliography

The Henry Moore Bibliography. Vol.1 1898–1986. Vol.2 1971–1986. Vol.3 Index 1898–1986. Vol.4 1986–1991. Vol.5 Index 1898–1991, ed. Alexander Davis, The Henry Moore Foundation, London and Much Hadham 1992–1994.

Catalogues raisonnés

Henry Moore: Complete Sculpture. Vol.1 1921–48 (entitled *Sculpture and Drawings*), ed. Herbert Read 1944, 4th revised edition ed. David Sylvester 1957. Vol.2 1949–54, ed. David Sylvester 1955, 3rd revised edition ed. Alan Bowness 1986. Vol.3 1955–64, ed. Alan Bowness 1965, 2nd revised edition 1986; reprinted 2005. Vol.4 1964–73, ed. Alan Bowness 1977. Vol.5 1974–80, ed. Alan Bowness 1983, 2nd revised edition 1994. Vol.6 1981–86, ed. Alan Bowness 1988. Lund Humphries, London.

Henry Moore: Catalogue of Graphic Work. [Vol.I] 1931–72, ed. Gérald Cramer, Alistair Grant and David Mitchinson 1973. Vol. II 1973–75, ed. Gérald Cramer, Alistair Grant and David Mitchinson 1976. Vol.III 1976–79, ed. Patrick Cramer, Alistair Grant and David Mitchinson 1980. Vol.IV 1980–84, ed. Patrick Cramer, Alistair Grant and David Mitchinson 1988. Cramer, Geneva.

Henry Moore: Complete Drawings. Vols. 1–7, ed. Ann Garrould, the Henry Moore Foundation in association with Lund Humphries, London, 1977–2003.

Books

Julian Andrews, *London's War: The Shelter Drawings of Henry Moore*, Lund Humphries, Aldershot 2002.

Roger Berthoud, *The Life of Henry Moore*, Faber, London 1987; revised edition Giles de la Mare, London 2003.

Anita Feldman, *Henry Moore Textiles*, introduction by Sue Prichard, Lund Humphries, London 2008.

Jeremy Lewison, *Moore*, Taschen, Cologne, 2007.

David Mitchinson (ed.), *Celebrating Moore, Works from the Collection of the Henry Moore Foundation*, selected and introduced by David Mitchinson with contributions from Julian Andrews, Roger Berthoud, Giovanni Carandente, Frances Carey, Anthony Caro, David Cohen, Susan Compton, Richard Cork, Penelope Curtis, Deborah Emont-Scott, Anita Feldman Bennet, Terry Friedman, Gail Gelburd, Clare Hillman, Phillip King, Christa Lichtenstern, Norbert Lynton, Bernard Meadows, Peter Murray, William Packer, John Read, Reinhard Rudolph, Julian Stallabrass, Julie Summers, Alan Wilkinson; Lund Humphries, London 1998; softback 2006 and 2008.

David Mitchinson (ed.), *Hoglands: The Home of Henry and Irina Moore*, essays by Anita Feldman Bennet, Andrew Causey, Martin Davis, Ann Garrould, Mary Moore, Michael Phipps, Lund Humphries, London 2007.

Alan Wilkinson, *Henry Moore Writings and Conversations*, Lund Humphries, London 2002.

An Introduction to Henry Moore, The Henry Moore Foundation, Much Hadham 2002; reprinted 2005.

Henry Moore's Sheep Sketchbook, comments by Henry Moore and Kenneth Clark, Thames and Hudson, London and New York 1980; revised edition 1998; reprinted 2008.

Sculpture in the Open Air at Perry Green, The Henry Moore Foundation, Much Hadham 1999; reprinted 2005.

Plaster *Reclining Mother and Child* (detail) 1975–76
photo: The Henry Moore Foundation archive

Recent exhibition catalogs

Henry Moore: The Challenge of Architecture, essays by Anita Feldman, David Mitchinson and Sarah Stanners, The Didrichsen Museum of Art and Culture, Helsinki 2008.

Moore at Kew, essay by Anita Feldman, Royal Botanic Gardens, London 2007.

Henry Moore et la Mythologie, essays by David Mitchinson, Anita Feldman, and Thierry Dufrène, Musée Bourdelle, Paris Musées 2007.

Henry Moore und die Landschaft, essays by Anita Feldman Bennet, Katja Blomberg, Beate Kemfert, Helmut Schmidt, and Irene Tobbin, Haus am Waldsee, Berlin, Opelvillen Rüsselheim, and DuMont Literatur und Kunst Verlag, Cologne 2007.

Henry Moore, essays by Anita Feldman Bennet, Maria Luisa Borràs, and Toby Treves, Fundació 'la Caixa', Barcelona 2006.

Henry Moore: Sculptuur en architectuur, essays by Anita Feldman Bennet, Jan van Adrichem and Suzanne Eustace, Terra, Rotterdam 2006.

Henry Moore: War and Utility, essays by David Mitchinson and Roger Tolson, Imperial War Museum, London 2006.

Henry Moore y Mexico, text by Toby Treves, Tate, and Museo Dolores Olmedo, Mexico City 2005.

Henry Moore: Epoche und Echo/Englische Bildhauerei im 20. Jahrhundert, essays by Ian Barker and Christa Lichtenstern, Swiridoff, Würth 2005.

Henry Moore: Uma Retrospectiva, essays by Aracy Amarel, Anita Feldman Bennet, Rafael Cadoso, David Mitchinson, and Margaret Reid, Pinacoteca do Estado de São Paulo; Paço Imperial, Rio de Janeiro; Centro Cultural Banco de Brasil, Brasília 2005.

Henry Moore: Human Landscapes/Menschliche Landschaften, essays by Christa Lichtenstern and Sabine Maria Aschmidt, Kerber Verlag, Bielefeld 2004.

Six Leading Sculptors and the Human Figure: Rodin, Bourdelle, Maillol, Brancusi, Giacometti, Moore, essays by Anita Feldman Bennet, Véronique Gautherin, Doïna Lemny, Bertrand Lorquin, Antoinette le Normand-Romain, Mary Lisa Palmer, National Gallery–Alexandros Soutzos Museum, Athens 2004.

Henry Moore, essays by Anita Feldman Bennet, Ian Dejardin, and Ann Garrould, Dulwich Picture Gallery; Scala, London 2004.

Henry Moore: Imaginary Landscapes, Frederik Meijer Gardens and Sculpture Park, Grand Rapids 2004.

Master Drawings from the Collection of the Henry Moore Foundation, Hazlitt Holland-Hibbert, London 2004.

Henry Moore: A Living Presence, essays by Anita Feldman Bennet and Koji Takahashi, Artis Inc, Tokyo 2003.

Moore: The Graphics, texts by Anita Feldman Bennet and David Mitchinson, the Henry Moore Foundation, Much Hadham 2003.

Henry Moore rétrospective, essays by Anita Feldman Bennet, Caroline Edde, Jean-Louis Prat, and Margaret Reid, Fondation Maeght, Saint Paul de Vence 2002.

Moore in China, text by David Mitchinson, the British Council, London and the Henry Moore Foundation, Much Hadham 2000.

Henry Moore: In the Light of Greece, essays by Anita Feldman Bennet and Roger Cardinal, Museum of Contemporary Art, Andros, Basil & Elise Goulandris Foundation 2000.

Moore in the Bagatelle Gardens, Paris, essay by David Cohen, photographs by Michel Muller, Lund Humphries, London 1992.

Plaster *Working Model for Reclining Figure: Angles* 1975–77
photo: The Henry Moore Foundation archive

"Sculpture is like a journey. You

return. The three-dimensiona

that a two-dimensional worlc

ave a different view as you

vorld is full of surprises in a way

buld never be." —Moore, 1962

Acknowledgments

The Board of The New York Botanical Garden would like to thank the Trustees and Director of the Henry Moore Foundation for lending works from their collection for this exhibition and to: David Mitchinson, Head of Collections & Exhibitions, and Anita Feldman, Curator, for making the selection and contributing a catalog essay; Charlotte Booth, Registrar, for coordinating the transport; Malcolm Woodward, James Copper, and Laura Robinson, Sculpture Conservators, for installation; and Suzanne Eustace, Assistant Curator, for writing the extended captions. Appreciation is also due to the following staff of the Henry Moore Foundation, who provided research and technical support: Pru Maxfield, Emma Stower, Emily Peters, and Rosemary Walker.

The Botanical Garden would also like to recognize the following for their services: Mariano Brothers; SpotCo; FGI Corporation; Darin Wacs; Masterpiece International, Ltd.; MOMART; Leone Design; Royal Botanic Gardens, Kew; Atlanta Botanical Garden; Arup; Metro Crane; Illuminations; Ruder Finn; Acoustiguide, Inc.; Hotel Thirty Thirty; Kraft Fence; Intaboro; Farrow & Ball; SAT, Inc.; Lighting by Gregory; and Concrete Express.

The Garden also acknowledges the efforts of many Horticulture division staff members in the success of the exhibition, including Todd Forrest, Karen Daubmann, Wayne Cahilly, Margaret Falk, Kurt Morrell, and Creative Services department staff members Mark Pfeffer and Ivo Vermeulen.

Front and back covers: *Oval with Points* 1968–70
Back cover foldout: *Oval with Points* (detail) 1968–70
photos: David Finn

Photos on pages 30–71: David Finn